CONTENTS

For men there was a new pastime of tweaking a cat's whisker – for women it was more important, as always, to decide what to wear for parties. Feminine fashion was now more daring and racy than ever before; the emancipated woman needed shorter dresses for the energetic dances of the time, and the new look included short hair, red lipstick, eye shadow and even coloured nail varnish (from 1925). Waterproof mascara was introduced by Elizabeth Arden and Helena Rubinstein in 1921. The popularity of cocktails fuelled the frivolous atmosphere of cabaret and carnival, while the tempo of jazz or Charleston shook the beaded dresses with their long fringes. From the early Twenties artificial silks had arrived in an increasing variety of prints; inexpensive and washable, fabrics like Rayon and Celanese enabled more young flappers to join the gaiety of night life. Rich fabrics were still the materials of the well-to-do – silk crêpe georgette, chiffon and satins, printed crêpe de chine and silk brocade – black and white outfits were seen as chic. As ever, fashion designers created the look of the decade – Paul Poiret (the first couturier to make his own range of perfumes and cosmetics), Coco Chanel (in 1921 her first perfume, Chanel Nº5, came to Britain), and Madeleine Vionnet, mistress of the bias cut.

Above, Debbie's evening outfit includes the Tutankamun-influenced handbag and the serpent head band with beaded tassels, and over her black chiffon dress she wears a silk lamé shawl with fringe. From 1923 the use of knitted sweaters, jumpers and cardigans became increasingly common for casual wear, as sported by the Prince of Wales when playing golf. Robert wears a sleeveless sweater whilst 'listening-in' on headphones connected to his Gecophone radio (Model Nº1 Type BC 1002 crystal set with glass enclosed cat's whisker in a mahogany box, made by the General Electric Co Ltd in 1922, £5.10s 0d.). Opposite the Gecophone is a three valve wireless set that would have cost around £35 in 1923; reception on valve sets was far better and they could pick up signals from a greater distance, although its formidable array of dials made it less straightforward to use. Outdoor or indoor aerials (above) were a prerequisite, and horn speakers enabled everyone to hear. In the early years, radios were battery powered. From 1925 'mains receivers' gradually came in, and by 1929 some speakers were being incorporated in the radio set – crystal sets were seen as obsolete.

INTRODUCTION

Returning to civilian life after the ravages of the Great War, ex-servicemen found massive unemployment (two million by 1922) and a housing shortage that left many war heroes reduced to sleeping on park benches and selling matches in the street. The British Legion was formed in 1921 and their poppy appeal began the same year, raising £106,000 to add to other funds supporting war veterans. For many Britons emigration to Empire countries was a fresh start; Australia offered a 'big brother movement' for boys (£5.10.0 fare for those under 17 years), while Canada was 'the new homeland'. The rise in communist sentiment matched the support for the Labour Party (founded in 1900), which formed a minority government in 1924 lasting just eight months, but returned in 1929. Meanwhile a general strike was called by the TUC in 1926 to back the coal miners; a million workers downed tools, but it only lasted nine days.

'The world's most wonderful exhibition', and the biggest ever was the British Empire Exhibition held at Wembley. Visitors were fascinated by the Queen's Dolls' House, a feat of miniaturisation right down to a working Singer sewing machine and a gramophone that played a record the size of a shilling. Also popular was the re-creation of Tutankamun's tomb that had been discovered by Howard Carter at Luxor, Egypt, in 1922.

As part of the Wembley complex, a stadium was built in time for the F.A. Cup final of 1923. The huge crowds spilled on to the pitch and a policeman on a white horse controlling the crowd became more famous than any of the players.

With women's right to vote won in 1918, there were still many other causes. Dr Marie Stopes opened the first birth control clinic in Britain in 1921, and there was increasing concern over animal rights – the League for the Prohibition of Cruel Sports was formed in 1924. Women found new emancipation in their shorter skirts, shorter hair, smoking in public (with elegant cigarette holders), and even powdering their noses in public.

Achieving new records on land, sea, rail and in the air, British technology was also in a race for television transmission; in the USA the first service began in May 1928, in Britain it was December 1928 using Logie Baird's system. (The world's first television journal was issued in March 1928.) In America a new era in cinema came in 1927 with Al Jolson in The Jazz Singer: the 'talkies' had arrived. In 1928 a new cartoon character, Mickey Mouse, began to rival the established favourite Felix the Cat.

Britons had reached every part of the globe, and almost the top of Everest, international air travel was taking off and so was motor car ownership (three times higher by 1929 thanks to hire purchase).

Instant mass communication had also arrived. Radio brought the voice of the king to six million of his subjects in 1924 for the first time. By the end of the decade there were 15 million listeners, but the news they heard was of the Wall Street crash and economic depression. At least there were many good books to read, from 'the book sensation' Metropolis to Ernest Hemingway's A Farewell to Arms, and for the youngsters A.A. Milne's Winnie-the-Pooh and friends.

The All-Electric House

How Electricity helps in the Quest for the Ideal Home

A Souvenir of The Ideal Home ... in 1920

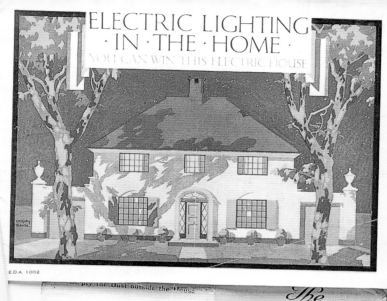

ELECTRIC LIGHTING IN THE HOME

YOU CAN WIN THIS ELECTRIC HOUSE

The WHIRLWIND

British and Best

MODERN Weekly 2d

BEGINS INSIDE

Cookery Number
No. 138. DECEMBER 8th, 1928.

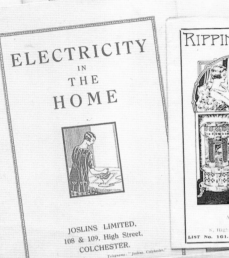

ELECTRICITY IN THE HOME

JOSLINS LIMITED,
108 & 109, High Street,
COLCHESTER.

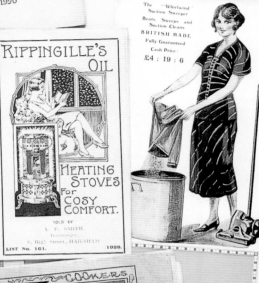

RIPPINGILLE'S OIL

HEATING STOVES For COSY COMFORT.

SOLD BY
A. E. SMITH,
8, High Street, HAILSHAM.
List No. 161. 1928.

The "Whirlwind" Suction Sweeper
Beats, Sweeps and Suction Cleans.
BRITISH MADE
Fully Guaranteed
Cash Price:
£4 : 19 : 6

Suction Sweeper

'Triplex'

The Grate that thousands of Housewives recommend

EWART'S GEYSERS in the Home

COLUMBIAN COOKERS

For Cleanliness, Comfort and Economy

"Oh, Mummie, it's lovely and Warm!"

T. T. NICHOLSON,
Pharmacist and Dispensing Chemist,
125, Hampstead Road,
N.W.1

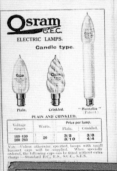

Osram G.E.C.
ELECTRIC LAMPS.
Candle type.

Osram LAMP

The Favourite

Fly through the day's work with a "Magnet" ELECTRIC CLEANER
Made in England

PYREX
MODERN COOKERY BOOK

VALOR PERFECTION OIL HEATERS
ROBSON BROS., ALNWICK.

VALOR PERFECTION OIL HEATER

MAPLE IDEAL HOMES 1928

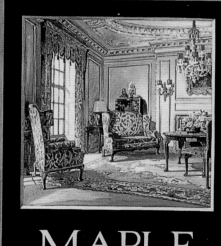

BEST BEDROOM OF HAMPTONS' NEW £175 HOUSE.

The building of houses had been neglected during the Great War, and thus in the early 1920s there was a great shortage. Idyllic homes on the coast at places like Peacehaven ('a short bus ride from the Aquarium, Brighton') or Kinmel Bay, N. Wales, lured families away from the city's dirt and grime'. Metro-land (served by the Metropolitan Railway) reached Croxley Green and Watford by 1925 — 'it is well wooded, well watered and wholly rural'.

For those lucky enough to have electricity in the home, electric lighting, heating and cooking now became possible, and also such luxuries as an electric kettle ('for the early morning cup of tea'), electric toaster ('without any scorching') and electric washing machine ('final banishment of washday drudgery'). An automatic electric refrigerator was another aspiration. According to Electrolux, the sensation of the 1927 Ideal Home Exhibition was their Motorless Refrigerator — without noise, attention or maintenance.

Ideal Home Bungalow-Cottage Second Bedroom

A HANDSOMELY furnished Bedroom in Walnut Queen Anne Style, the furniture being enriched with figured burr fronts. Shown at the Ideal Home Exhibition, 1928.

Furniture for Four-room House or Flat for £72
OR COMPLETELY FURNISHED for £125.

FURNISHING SCHEMES Nos. 1 and 2.
ON VIEW IN OUR GALLERIES.

THIS Living Room is included in our £125 and £200 Complete Furnishing Schemes. Scheme No. 1

During the Twenties, there was a steady flow of new brands.
Notable launches included Smith's Crisps in 1920 (adding a
blue paper twist of salt in 1922), Wall's Ice Cream in 1922 along with the familiar 'Stop me and buy one'
tricycles, and Lyons vacuum-packed coffee went on sale in 1920. From 1925 Shredded Wheat was made

at Welwyn Garden City showing the new factory on the carton.
Packaging design was changing; for instance, Lux updated its Victorian look for a 'deco' style in 1925. Products kept up-to-date in other ways.
Huntley & Palmers manufactured Jackie Coogan biscuits, Macfarlane Lang produced Broadcast cake, Charlie Chaplin appeared on Kinema
toffee, Mary Pickford on Kinema Krunchies, and sweet assortments caught the mood of the moment, where Lyons Gala Night or Slade's Gaiety.

7.

In the days before their emancipation a few headstrong women had smoked in private, but with so many new freedoms gained, an increasing number began to delight in the habit, and society had to accept it. By the end of the decade, women accounted for nearly 5% of cigarette sales. Exotic blends were favoured by this new breed of flapper-girls (as above for Star cigarettes, launched in 1923). Turkish, Egyptian, Russian and Havana were all blends included in the mixed box of Blue Book (right). Cigarette cards were also becoming more diverse. Prince Charming cigarettes used a photograph of the Prince of Wales, but carefully removed the cigarette he smoked.

LISTENIN'!
"Stand by one minute please, and you will hear the lions roar!"

LISTENIN'!
"Come to the party - but bring your own headphones!"

LISTENIN'!
"Hi! Just broadcast to my Bill at the 'Crown and Anchor,' that if 'e aint 'ome in ten minutes, there's trouble brewing!"

LISTENIN'!
dere Mr. Broadcaster:
"Will you like me to kum up and sing for you my young man says my voice is that eavenerly that I ought to be on the pictures!"

LISTENIN'!
"Stand by everybody you will now hear the familiar cry of a night Owl"

LISTENIN'!
"You've got them clothes lines a bit too 'igh Sir!!"

"I can distinctly hear Titums."

IF YOU'RE GOING IN FOR **WIRELESS** IT'S ADVISABLE TO HAVE YOUR **AERIALS** ON THE ROOF AT HOME

Dear Mother,
I am sending you ten shillings - next week - - - by WIRELESS.

"I CAN PICK UP MOST PLACES WITH MY OLD VALVE SET, BUT I'M BLOWED IF I'VE MANAGED TO PICK YOU UP YET!"

Operatic Number
(You are Queen of My Heart to Night)

LISTENING IN.
And they call this Wireless

"A smart 'bob' always catches 'em."

"To 'bob' or not to 'bob' - That is the question!"

"The nearer the 'bob' the sweeter the meat!"

The Greeting is "Short"
I send "Bobbing" along,
But it carries a "Crop"
of Good Wishes.
May Christmas be jolly
with music and song,
And heaps of
good things
on the dishes.
Best Wishes

Skirts have grown shorter
For Mother and Daughter.
When it blows,
Each one shows
A bit more than she oughter.

"Her husband can't make both ends meet - but she comes jolly near doing it!"

WHAT WITH ME BOBBED HAIR AND RUSSIAN BOOTS, I LOOK LIKE CLICKING THIS SEASON!

I FEEL LIKE A BALLY RUSSIAN IN THE RUSSIAN BALLET— SO CHASE ME BOYS, I'M FULL O' BEANSKI!

WHAT EVER NEXT?

"Wear longer skirts Mummy! Do you want me to look like a Monk?"

"Fancy their bringing that squalling kid to the wedding! When I get married I shall put on the invitation cards - "No babies expected"!!"

"Life is a story!"
"Yes, dear, divided into Chap 1, Chap 2, Chap 3 and the others!"

HOW DO YOU LIKE THE FLOOR?

BOBS AN' SHINGLES ARE OUT OF DATE, SO DO GROW YOUR TRESSES, DEAR—QUICK I'SE BOUGHT A TAIL—I COULDN'T WAIT—BUT—I CAN'T GET THE THING TO STICK!

EVEN A WORM WILL TURN!

Comic picture postcards reflected the life and times of the Twenties — humorous situations around the new wireless sets, the latest fashions for short hair and shorter dresses, and all the fun on the dance floor.

Opposite page. The film cartoon character, Felix, was drawn onto postcards and made out he was better than Chaplin, Fairbanks or Valentino. The Daily Mirror's Pip, Squeak and Wilfred come out to play; and a selection of character dogs drawn by George Studdy appear - his main dog Bonzo had been developed by 1922 (see also pp 28-29).

10.

"In dancing the Black Bottom - don't let your right hip know what your left hip's doing!"

GOT IT!

"I think the weaker sex is often the stronger sex - - because of the weakness of the stronger sex for the weaker sex!"

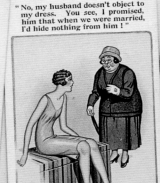

"No, my husband doesn't object to my dress. You see, I promised, him that when we were married, I'd hide nothing from him!"

"They're off!"
GREYHOUND TO-NIGHT RACING

"EVERY DOG—I MEAN CAT—HAS HIS DAY. THERE'S FAIRBANKS, CHAPLIN, VALENTINO, AND OTHERS, ALL CRYING THEIR EYES OUT 'COS I'M IT!"

SWANK FELIX!

"Felix, what is your wave length?"

"Do you really mean all you say, Felix?"

Oh! Felix—"Last night on the back porch!"

"If you can't be good Felix—be careful!"

"I'm surprised at you Felix!"

"Please Lord, excuse me while I kick Felix!"

"Felix, a little of what you fancy'll do you good!"

"Love all" indeed! Wish I dare use a swear word!"

"Felix is the hope of our side!"

"If I could only express my feelings!"

"So near - and yet so far!"

WE'RE FOREVER BLOWING BUBBLES

A LITTLE PAINT MAKES A BIG DIFFERENCE

A SLOW GAME

HOW D'YOU DO?

NEARING THE END OF A PERFECT DAY!

There's room for two or three more, so why not come

"THERE YOU ARE THEN!"

IT WAS A BIT OF A FIGHT GETTING HERE, BUT NOW WE ARE HERE IT'S WORTH IT. IT'S LOVELY

Say When.

We are a Sporty Little Crowd down here.

Such Stuff as Dreams are made of.

Somewhere the Sun is Shining.

We met several Road Hogs on our way down.

Swank.

Rabbits, I Believe?

That's What I think of You.

The Beggars Opera.

The End of a Perfect Day.

Now what about it?

William Tell.

HAIR DRESSING
Styles
—told in Pictures 6ᴰ

Hair Dressing Styles
specially arranged
—Messrs SELFRIDGE & Cᵒ Ltd

Weldons
HOME MILLINER
Nᵒ 152
3ᴰ

This shape of the New

The "Erica" Hat

"Best Way" Series, No. 61

Shall I Bob It or Leave It Long?

"MUL-KOH" SHINGLING CLIPPER

FINEST QUALITY

CUTS

THE GLORY OF A WOMAN'S
NOT WHAT SHE HAS BU
SHE DOES WITH

When Weary of Bobbed Hair Just

JACKIE COOGAN in "Circus Days."

Picture Show
Every Monday 2½
Vol. 9. No. 234.   OCTOBER 20th, 1923.

How Famous Film Stars Invest their Earnings

Special Article Inside.

PRISCILLA DEAN

MARY PICKFORD

GOOD LOOKS!

HOME NOTES

No. 1620. APRIL 4, 1925. Price 2d. Vol. CXXVI.

Lady Kitty Vincent—Berta Ruck—write inside

HOME CHAT

Has Your Beauty an Age Lin

HOME CHA

Nash's
and Pall Mall Magazine
May 1/- Nett

Easter Fiction Number

2ᴰ

DON'T WEAR THAT FLO
HOME CHA
Vol. CXXIX. No. 1680.

The close-fitting cloche hat made its
appearance in 1924; also in vogue
were the bandanna and the Tam
O'Shanter. The new cloche hat
required short hair, bobbed, cropped
or shingled into permanent waves
and curls. There were many
variations on the theme, such as
the Peter Pan shingle 'which is
curled so attractively and gives such
a charming line to the head'. Film
stars both set the fashions, or had
to follow them — Mary Pickford cut
her long tresses eventually. Louise
Brooks became known for her bob
of ebony hair and kiss curl (right).

12.

The look of the 1920s was sleek and straight. For several years, women had shown their ankles, but now more leg was revealed and hemlines soared to just below the knee by 1925-6 - for a daring few it went further, with Donald McGill's saucy postcards making fun of the revelations (see p.10 and 58). Bosoms were flattened in order to achieve the new shape, and many took to slimming aids, or at least a lot of dancing. The final resort was the new elastic girdle that flattened those parts of the figure previous corsets had emphasised. Along with fur collars and trimmings, artificial silks with printed patterns were everywhere; hard wearing and easily washed, they were available at 'a price women can hardly believe'.

14.

The Twenties blew in with the fox trot, tango and a rage for jazz and mask parties. Another Latin American dance followed, the Paso Doble, and there were brief flirtations with the Jog Trot, Twinkle, Vampire and Shimmy. But by 1925 it was the Charleston from the USA that shook out the rest. In 1927 another dance, the Black Bottom, kept dancing instructors busy (see p.1). Tins for toffee and sweet assortments caught the tempo.

Christmas time was carnival time, with lots of fancy dress balls. By 1925 the vogue was for costumes that were colourful, bright, but cool for dancing. Some could afford a different outfit for each occasion, others made do with one fancy dress costume to last through the season. It was 'bad form to spend a lot of money on ostentatious and expensive costumes.' Competitions were held for the best homemade outfit costing under ten shillings.

16.

THE PRETTIEST BLOUSE SLIP PATTERN FREE!

WOMAN'S LIFE
This Pattern Inside

PRICE THREEPENCE.   No. 503 (New Serial)   SEPTEMBER 24,

PALS, October 9, 1922.

REAL PHOTO OF LIVERPOOL F.C. INSIDE.

MYSTERY SPORT ADVENTURE

Pals

EVERY 2d. MONDAY

VOL. I.—No. 1.   [Registered for Transmission By Canadian Magazine Post.]   OCTOBER 9, 1922.

LONDON

No. 215.   Saturday, March 8.

LADY GRANT on SHOULD SOCIETY WOMEN WORK? inside

"QUALITY & FLAVOUR."   BOURNVILLE COCOA   MADE UNDER IDEAL CONDITIONS.
See the name "CADBURY" on every piece of Chocolate.

HOME CHAT
AND MOTHER & HOME
Every 2d. Monday

Business Girls' Number

THE HOME COMPANION 2d.

"To Have—and to Hold"

CHILDREN'S MUSIC PORT. PA FOLIO

WOMAN'S W
The Favourite Paper of a Mi

No. 1,001.   EVERY MONDAY.

No. 1   THE NEW PAPER FOR EVERY HOUSEWIFE   No. 1

HOME MAKING
and Home Cookery
3d.

OF MATRIMONY

and forsaking all
other, keep thee
only unto her so
long as ye bo
shall live

This Soul-Gripping St
Begins Next Week

T.P.'s and Cassell's Weekly—October 27, 1923.   THE BOOK OF THE WEEK. By T.P.

T.P.'s and Cassell's Weekly
Edited by T.P. O'Connor, M.P.

Vol. I—No. I. (NEW SERIES)   OCTOBER 27, 1923.   [Registered at the G.P.O. as a Newspaper, and for Canadian Post.]   Price 2d.

We Des

HO NO

GREAT
The Only
"CUT-OUT A

1,341.

BRIGHTER LONDON

VOL. I. No. 1.   FRIDAY, NOVEMBER 3, 1922.   TWOPENCE

MYSTIC EASTERN PERFUME SACHET INSIDE!

Love Stories
2d. Every Saturday
Vol. I. No. 3.   November 16th, 1923

FREE Pattern of My Special Jumper with No. 1

Olive Wadsley's Weekly
2d.

Stories of Love and Romance

Elinor Glyn
Ruby M. Ayres
Berta Ruck

My New Ser

THE HUMORIST
IN VARIOUS MOODS

No. 1. Vol. I.   JULY 29, 1922.   Registered as a Newspaper and for the Canadian Post.   Two Pence

SIDE-SPLITTING NEW SERIAL   COMMENCES NEXT WEEK! ORDER YOUR COPY EARLY!

Sports Fun 2d
THE ONE LONG LAUGH PAPER

SO I DID!

GOOD GRACIOUS STEVE! I THOUGHT YOU WERE GOING TO REFEREE!

ZARAH'S MAGIC CRYSTAL FREE INSIDE

Pam's Paper 2d.
No. 1.—Dec. 1, 1923   Every Week.   Registered for Transmission by Canadian Magazine Post.

No. 1 OF GREAT NEW STORY PAPER

28-page BEAUTY BOOK FREE—INSIDE

POPPY'S PAPER 2d
EVERY MONDAY

Passionate Surrender

No. 1   Feb. 2, 1924

No. 1 of a N

CH

No. 1

LIFE 2ᴰ

No¹ of **JOY** The LOVE and LAUGHTER Weekly — EVERY TUESDAY — 2ᴰ
Feb. 14, 1925

SPECIAL SPRING FASHION NUMBER
Woman's Way
Not for to-morrow
For happiness pray
Make happiness certain
And grasp it to-day.
VOL. 2 25ᵀᴴ FEB. 1928 No 26 PRICE 2ᴰ

No. 1. GREAT NEW HOME PAPER
WOMAN'S FRIEND
PRICE 2ᴰ
This Pattern Free Inside
Would he discover that the child was not theirs?
PRIZE OF £3 A WEEK FOR LIFE!

MODERN Weekly 2ᴰ
No. 1
Free inside
This Clark
and DOUBLE SHEET
APRIL 17th, 1924.

ALL FOR SHOW. ROMANTIC LONG NOVEL COMPLETE INSIDE.
Betty's Paper 2ᴰ
VOL. X.—No. 235. MAY 21, 1927
EVERY SATURDAY
Lucky Lingerie Set

1/3

2ᴰ

GOLDEN CHARM FREE TO-DAY — No. 1 NEW HOME PAPER
No¹ SEP. 14 1929 PRICE 2ᴰ
RED STAR Weekly
The New Story Paper
The TRUE STORY of CORA CRIPPEN NOW TOLD FOR THE FIRST TIME

and Cut — You Simply Sew

No. 1 of Great New Weekly
EVERY SATURDAY TWOPENCE
REGISTERED FOR TRANSMISSION BY CANADIAN MAGAZINE POST.
Up-to-Date
The Paper for the Smart Woman
No. 1.—Vol. 1. MAY 21 1927
"CLOSED FOR REPAIRS"
Patent Needle-Threader Free Inside This Copy.

Feminine Life
Vol. 14. No. 8. AUGUST, 1928 Price Twopence

ATURE
kly with a O-MAKE UP"

'No. 1 OF THE MARRIED WOMAN'S OWN PAPER'
WOMAN'S COMPANION 2ᴰ
No. 1 EVERY SATURDAY. November 5th, 1927
Free Packet of Delicious AUSTRALIAN SULTANAS and this Cookery Book INSIDE!
FLOUR
Dried Fruit Cookery

RM 2ᴰ
1925 Every Saturday
Poudre d'orsay
FREE PACKET of FACE POWDER INSIDE

London Calling. Vol. 1. No. 1. March 3rd, 1928.
LONDON CALLING
WIT AND GOSSIP OF THE WEEK
2ᴰ WEEKLY
H.R.H. as seen by HYNES
P. G. WODEHOUSE ~ W. J. LOCKE ~ ROSITA FORBES
EDGAR WALLACE ~ BEVERLEY NICHOLS

A vast choice of 2d. periodicals with which to while away idle moments. Romantic story papers told of 'the great love between a white maid and her arab captor' and Eve's Own presented a colour picture of Valentino and Swanson in their first number, 1923 (see p.3). More general home papers discussed the perennial topic of 'will men and women ever understand one another?' In the first issue of Modern (1924) there was reflection on 'sleep secrets', 'marriage or career', and a health club in London where fashionable women go for daily exercise. The Humorist (1922) was there to add a little wit.

SUNDAY AT HOME
Edited By KENNEDY WILLIAMSON

Good Housekeeping
AUGUST, 1928
ONE SHILLING
NETT

No.1 *of the* NEW *Illustrated Weekly*
The Looker-On

THE
WOMAN'S
MAGAZINE
EDITED BY
FLORA KLICKMANN

VOGUE

TWO CHARMING BABY PAINTINGS *inside*
Wife and Home
6d
MONTHLY

JULY
NY MAG.

LONDON
OPINION
6d

SIXPENCE
JANUARY 1928
EVERY GIRL'S PAPER
INCORPORATING THE "C.C."

No 1
The Magazine
for the
Young Wife
October, 1929
BEFORE BABY COMES"
In-Natal Articles by a Doctor
8 page
CHILDREN'S FASHIONS
ROTOTONE Supplement
WIVES' HEALTH
Questions Answered
How to Make
BABY'S FIRST WOOLLIES
EVERY HOUSEHOLD
BEAUTY ARTICLES
Complete Stories
"Opening Chapters of
HUNGRY HEART
by
Joan Kingston

No Re

HOUSE
WOMAN 1/net
CULTURE·HEALTH·HOME DECORATION·FASHIONS·FICTION

Are You A Three-Job Woman?
MODERN WOMAN
FEBRUARY
6d

NSTRUCTIVE · ENTERTAINING

More substantial magazines with
colourful covers cost from 6d to 2/-.
Their illustrations were created by
artists like Barribal (cover of Pan,
where a young woman dares to smoke
a cigarette), Rilette for the monthly
magazine Woman, and Wilton William
giving a risqué look to the new illustrated
weekly Looker-On. From the USA, Good
Housekeeping arrived in 1924 to join
Vogue (in Britain since 1916). Specialist
magazines catered for many ideas.
Open Air was for lovers of nature
and outdoor life, with articles on
'the envy of the slow', 'comfort for the
camper' and 'the wonder of the woods'.
The Happy Mag made sure that all
their stories had a happy ending. Modern
Woman of 1928 (launched 1925) was able
to ponder over 'Women police - are they
a failure?' and that motherhood was
no longer a complete bar to a career. 21.

Secrets of Muscle Control.

APRIL

Health
AND EFFICIENCY

6d

'Ware the Medicine Monger!

Tonsils & Adenoids: Nature *versus* Knife

Cross Country Running for Health.

Try these Outdoor Games—Indoors!

Art Plates of STEWART ROME and VIRGINIA V...

Picture Show

Every Monday 2d

Vol. 11 No. ... AUGUST 23rd, 1924.

How to Improve Your Tennis

EXPLAINED ON THE SCREEN BY KITTY McKANE

SPECIAL ARTICLE INSIDE

KITTY McKANE

Demonstrating to the film photographer

SPORT'S BIGGEST THRILL!

Dog Racing

2d

The Only Paper in the World solely devoted to Greyhound and Whippet Racing

Vol. I. [LINE HOUSE, 34-35, WHITE LANE, LONDON, E.C.] SATURDAY, MAY 28, 1927 [Registered at the G.P.O. as a Newspaper and for Canadian Magazine Post.] No. 1.

SATURD...

GIVE YOUR DOGS "BENBOW" AND KEEP THEM FIT

THE SPORTING GREYHOUND

With which is incorporated "The Greyhound."

A JOURNAL DEVOTED TO GREYHOUND RACING

No. 1. VOL. 1 [Registered at the G.P.O. as a newspaper] AUGUST 20th, 1927. [Postage U.K. newspaper rate]

GREYHOUND RACING

2d WEEKLY   2d WEEKLY

VOL. 1, No. 7 [Registered as a Newspaper] Aug. 20th, 1927

FREE CUP-TIE PLATE! £500 PRIZE OFFER!

SPORTS BUDGET
AND FOOTBALL SPECIAL

2d Vol. I. No. 1. January 13th, 1923

Great One Week contest

£500

MUST BE WON!

THE SCOTTISH CUP

Special Cup-Tie Number

...AL FOOTBALL NUMBER.

THE FINEST ADVENTURE WEEKLY

Scout

2d

FOUNDED BY SIR ROBERT BADEN-POWELL B.T

...AW OF KITTY'S. | "HOW TO GET GOALS."
...al Serial by Michael Foole | Full-ol-Tips Footer Article by Charlie Buchan
October 15, 1927. | PRICE TWOPENCE.

THE ILLUSTRATED SPORTING WORLD, SATURDAY, MARCH 16, 1929.

CARPENTIER'S CONFESSIONS See page 4

The ILLUSTRATED SPORTING WORLD
2d WEEKLY

Incorporating STAGE AND FILM PICTORIAL

THIS WEEK
LORD DECIES
GEORGES CARPENTIER
H. A. VACHELL
H. M. ABRAHAMS
LADY ALLAN HORNE
MARY PICKFORD
GEORGE DUNCAN

No. 1 SATURDAY, MARCH 16th, 1929 [Registered at the G.P.O. as a Newspaper]

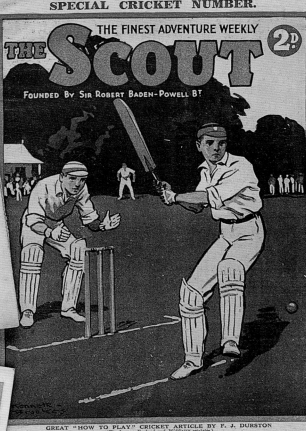

SPECIAL CRICKET NUMBER.

THE FINEST ADVENTURE WEEKLY

THE Scout

2d

FOUNDED BY SIR ROBERT BADEN-POWELL B.T

GREAT "HOW TO PLAY" CRICKET ARTICLE BY F. J. DURSTON
(The famous England and Middlesex cricketer.)

No. 1105. Vol. XXIV. June 29, 1929. PRICE TWOPENCE.

Weldon's Socks & Stockings for Men & Boys

6d

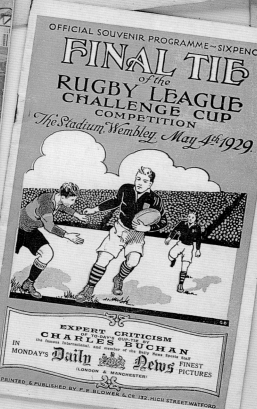

OFFICIAL SOUVENIR PROGRAMME ~ SIXPENCE

FINAL TIE
of the
RUGBY LEAGUE
CHALLENGE CUP
COMPETITION

The Stadium, Wembley, May 4th, 1929.

EXPERT CRITICISM
OF TO-DAY'S CUP-TIE
BY
CHARLES BUCHAN
the famous International, and member of the Daily News Sports Staff

IN
Monday's Daily News
(LONDON & MANCHESTER)

FINEST PICTURES

PRINTED & PUBLISHED BY F. E. BLOWER & Co. 132 HIGH STREET, WATFORD.

The world of sport was well represented by a variety of periodicals, from the Cricket Enthusiast (1922) to Sporting World (1929). In 1926 greyhound racing events began in the UK, and within six months their appeal was able to support three papers (see above). Women were able to play tennis or golf with greater ease, helped by the fashion for a rising hemline. Indeed, encouraged by advice from magazines and slow motion film instruction at Gaumont cinemas, tennis became a respectable way of finding a partner. Women's football teams were popular, and Football Favourite included an article on 'Can girls play football?' Some magazines offered the chance to win up to £500 for the forecast closest to the results of twelve football matches.

23

A WEEKLY PAPER FOR THE TINY TOTS.

THE CHICKS' OWN 2d

No. 1.   EVERY TUESDAY.   September 25th, 1920.

AN IDEAL GIFT BOOK FOR BOYS AND GIRLS: "THE PLAYBOX ANNUAL" NOW ON SALE.

TigerTim's WEEKLY. 1½

No. 52.   Vol. 2.   January 22, 1921.

THE FUNNY ADVENTURES OF THE BUMPTY BOYS.

A Little Mouse Causes a Lot of Trouble in School.

GLOSSY PHOTO
Manchester United
R. Gillespie, Queen
Issued This We

Adve

THE 12
GRAND SERIES OF
No 215. - 24th OCT. 192

PICTURES, MORE PICTURES, EVEN MORE PICTURES AND THEN SOME !!!

The All Picture Comic 2d

No. 1. Vol. I.   THE PAPER YOU CAN TAKE HOME.   March 12, 19—

...NESS.

SIX TRANSFERS FREE WITH THIS NUMBER !

THE MONSTER COMIC 1d

No. 1.   Vol. I.   PRICE ONE PENNY—EVERY MONDAY.   23rd September, 19 2.

WIRELESS WILLIE & BERTIE BROADCAST

FREE POCKET MONEY FOR YOU. See page 17.

The British Girl 2d

No. 1.

FREE POCKET MONEY FOR BOYS : See page 19.

The British Boy 2d

No. 1. Vol. I.   EVERY FRIDAY.   July 23, 1921.

THE SUNBEAM 2d
A Bright Paper for Children.

A LOVELY TOY BALLOON INSIDE

THE SUNBEAM 2d

A JOLLY
Picture & Story Paper
for BOYS & GIRLS
EVERY TUESDAY • Price Twopence

Vol. I. No. 1.   October 7th, 1922.

A VOYAGE TO THE MO—

Boys Maga

TOBY

Amusing : Attractive : Artistic

MONTHLY   EDITED BY G. HEATH ROBINSON

Vol. I. No. 1.   SEPTEMBER, 1921.

SIX COLOURED TRANSFERS GIVEN AWAY FREE

THE GOLDEN COMIC 1d

Every Monday

No. 1. Vol. I.   Companion Paper to "THE MONSTER 1d. COMIC."   14th October, 1922.

DANIEL DOLE & OSCAR OUTOFWORK.

GREAT NEW ADVENTURE

No 1
The
Biggest
STORY
WEEKLY
The
World!

Vol. I. No. 1.

PICTURES AND STORIES FOR BOYS AND GIRLS OF ALL AGES, ALL

LITTLE SPARKS 1½d

CHAMPION
REAL PHOTOS of FAMOUS CHAMPIONS EVERY WEEK !

The CHAMPION 2d

MYSTERY-ADVENTURE-SPORT
The Tip-Top Story Weekly

No. 1. Vol. I.   EVERY MONDAY.   Week ending January 28th, 1922.

2d   BUBBLES   BIG COLOURED BALLOON INSIDE !

BUBBLES

AND THE CHILDREN'S FAIRY

No. 1. Vol. I.   EVERY THURSDAY. PRICE TWOPENCE.   April 16th, 1921.

A BIG BRIGHT BUDGET OF TIP-TOP STORIES

PLUCK 2d

The Great
SPORT & ADVENTURE
STORY-PAPER

Vol. 1. No. 5.   Companion Paper to THE CHAMPION.   EVERY TUESDAY.   Week Ending Nov. 25th, 1922.

ALL THESE PRIZES GIVEN AW—

YOUNG BRIT

EVERY THURSDAY

YOU MUST NOT MISS OUR GRAND NEW SERIAL "DOREEN, THE CIRCUS STAR !"

No. 178. Vol. 7.   Week Ending October 14th, 192

The School Friend 2d

Every Thursday

OUR GRAND CHRISTMAS NUMBER !

The Schoolgirls' Own

FREE GIFT OF SHARP'S KREEMY

The Schoolgirl 1½d

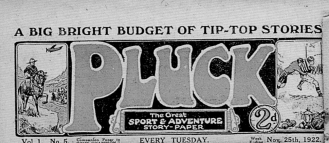

FOOTBALLERS
Solve these P
and WIN

4 School Stories—New Highwayman Serial "B

Week Ending
January 19th,
1924.
New
Series.
No. 201.

The POPUL

The Story Paper
for Boys.

Twentyeight
Pages.

EVERY
TUESDA

No. 1 of Grand New Paper ! Fine Stories ! Free Footballs !

SCHOOL AND SPORT 1½d

Published
EVERY MONDAY

o. 1. Vol. I.   Week ending DECEMBER 17th, 1921.   PRICE 1½d

EDITED BY
H. A. HINTON.

THE BEST PAPER FOR BOYS !

The BOYS' HERALD 2d

No. 92.   ON SALE EVERY TUESDAY.   July 30, 1921.

Billy Bunter
in the Football Field

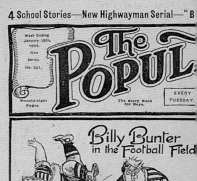

Even though the Great War had recently run its course, the board games of Dover Patrol, Aviation and Tri-Tactics were compelling games for adults and children. Amongst toy trains, two new developments came on track. Following the continued success of Meccano, Frank Hornby decided to market a 'toy railway system'. In 1920 his Hornby clockwork train was launched, being put together on the Meccano principle that 'much pleasure can be derived from taking them all to pieces and refashioning them'. An example of a boxed set is displayed above. In the event, it was found that boys did not appreciate a train that could come to pieces, and by

the time of the first Hornby
Book of Trains in 1925 (p56 centre),
the trains were constructed without nuts and bolts. In 1922, the
German toy manufacturer, Bing, pioneered a small gauge miniature railway for the table top (see above).
Amongst dolls, Nora Wellings began in 1926; her 'islander doll' with glass eyes sits above. Topical toys: greyhound racing, wireless operator, R100 airship.

Competition amongst national newspapers was intense. The Daily Express, News Chronicle and Daily Herald had all reached a million circulation by the end of the 1920s, and the Daily Mail was close to two million. (By 1924 The News of the World was selling three million each Sunday) To entertain the children, the D.Mail had introduced a comic character called Teddy Tail in 1915, drawn by Charles Folkard in a series of nine panels each day. Then in 1919 the D.Mirror put in its children's section a four-frame panel featuring a dog and a penguin, Pip and Squeak. In 1920 a baby rabbit, Wilfred, joined the story drawn by A.B.Payne. The Pip and Squeak give-away comic began in 1921 (till 1925), the annual in 1923 followed by Wilfred's in 1924. In 1927 the Wilfredian League of Gugnuncs (WLoG) was founded; members of this 'secret society' were known as Gugnuncs (two words in Wilfred's limited vocabulary, 'gug' and 'nunc'). Not wanting to miss out, the D.Express introduced Mary Tourtell's creation Rupert Bear in 1920, initially as a single

panel story each day. The first compilation of the stories was published in 1924 (see left). The Daily Sketch began a cartoon strip featuring Pop in 1921, a good-humoured man who over time lost his hair and gained a paunch. The strip was drawn by J. Millar Watt; the annuals appeared from 1925. Other children's strips included the Noah Family in the Daily News from 1919, Oojah the elephant in the D. Sketch children's supplement, and Bobby Bear in the D. Herald from around 1919. Dismal Desmond was the creation of Dean's Rag Book Co. and like Bonzo (see also p.11) was used in advertisements. Felix the Cat was the creation of Otto Messmer in 1920; his film cartoon character quickly achieved worldwide appeal. The popularity of the Bruin Boys and especially Tiger Tim had started with the Rainbow comic in 1914 (see also p 24-5), but there were many challengers to this crowd of anthropomorphic characters, not least the books of A.A. Milne with E.H. Shepard's illustrations. Christopher Robin with his teddy bear, Pooh, and friends Piglet, Eeyore, Kanga, Rabbit and Owl appeared in Winnie-the-Pooh in 1926 and The House at Pooh Corner (1928), and as soft toys (above). **29**

This is our Special DOROTHY DALTON Number.

picture plays 2d

Vol. 1. No. 39. August 14th, 1920.

The OCTOBER
Picturegoer
Monthly 1/net
VOL. 2. No. 10 1921

Jackie Coogan

"SAFETY LAST."
Splendid Pictorial Article of Harold Lloyd's finest...

PICTURE-PLAY
NOV. 1924 MAGAZINE 25 Cents

...nty Big Pages and a Plate of "FATTY" ARBUCKLE. C.

Film Fun. 1½d

No. 1. Vol. 1. January 17, 1920.

THE ADVENTURES of
WINKLE
THE PATHÉ MIRTH WIZARD
...INTO THINGS FOR A START.

5/- A DAY FOR SIX MONTHS !!

The Kinema Comic 1½d
(with which is incorporated CHEERIO!)

No. 1. Vol. 1. (Every Wednesday.) April 24, 1920.

The Funniosities of
Fatty Arbuckle.
The Famous-Lasky Star
This week's Film : "CUT OUT FOR THE JOB."

Movie-Land
PRICE 6d.

REGISTERED AT G.P.O.
AS A NEWSPAPER
No. 1. VOL. 1.
Jan 3rd 1921.

A NEW YEAR PRIZE OFFER TO ALL READERS!

1922 **Funny Wonder.** NEW YEAR No. 1 1½d

No. 407. WITH THE "FUNNY WONDER" IS NOW INCORPORATED "FUNNY CUTS," "THE WORLD'S COMIC," and "SMILER." JANUARY 7, 1922.

CHARLIE CHAPLIN · KING of the KINEMA

No. 924. Vol. LIX.
THE
BIO
Copyright
Registered at the...

...POSTCARD MAY BRING YOU A FOO...

BOYS' CIN...
...95. VOL. 8. SEPTEMBER 1st, 1923. EVERY WEDNESDAY.

THE
KINEMATOGRAPH
WEEKLY
Registered at the G.P.O. as a Newspaper.

With more and more moving pictures, mostly from
America, going to the movies had become an
established part of weekly entertainment.
Adventure in the wild west was led by Tom Mix,
while the daring deeds of a hero dog were
played by Rin-Tin-Tin. The eight-year-old
Jackie Coogan was an instant hit in The Kid
(1921) playing opposite Charlie Chaplin — it was
Chaplin's first full-length feature film. Women
swooned over the dashing looks of Rudolf
Valentino or Ronald Colman; for men there were
the dazzling vamps and flappers. An endless
supply of film magazines kept everyone's
favourite film star close at hand. But it
was the arrival of the 'talkie' in 1927 that
transformed the appeal of picture-going;
starring Al Jolson, The Jazz Singer claimed
the honours for breaking the silence.

THE GREAT RE-ISSUE
of
Mary Pickford
in

WALTURDAW
FIRST NATIONAL

"Daddy Long Legs"
THE WONDER PRODUCTION
THAT HAS BROKEN
ALL RECORDS.

BRITISH EXHIB...
(1922) prese...
MILDRED...
The DEC...

CHARLES CHAPLIN
in "The Pilgrim".
...Pictures of latest comedy...

Wireless Review

3^d

No. I.   Vol. I.   JUNE 2, 1923

Wireless Weekly

CAPTAIN
and Wireless Supplement

№1 *'All about Wireless"- A New Paper for ALL*

POPULAR WIRELESS
3d

No. I Vol. I   June 3 1922

Weekly

DISTANT LISTENING. By Captain Eckersley.
World-Radio, April 8, 1927.

WORLD-RADIO
BBC
AND FOREIGN

DOMINION   PROGRAMMES

WITH WHICH IS INCORPORATED "THE RADIO SUPPLEMENT"

CONSTRUCTIONAL—HUMOROUS—DRAMATIC—EXPLANATORY

The Wireless Magazine

Edited by
Bernard E. Jones   VOL.1; NO.1.   February 1925
One Shilling

ECONOMIC *Radio* ELECTRIC

MARCONI GREETS US (p. 3) :: THREE WIRELESS SETS GIVEN AWAY (p. 16)

OUR FIRST NUMBER

Amateur Wireless
And Electrics

No. 1   SATURDAY, JUNE 10, 1922   Price 3d

MODERN WIRELESS
February.

THE LARGEST BRITISH WIRELESS MAGAZINE

L. I. No. I.   Edited by JOHN SCOTT-TAGGART, F.Inst.P., Member I.R.E.   February, 1923.
1/-

"WIRELESS," OCTOBER 3, 1925.   [Registered at the G.P.O. as a Newspaper]

WIRELESS
2d
THE ONE—WORD WEEKLY

Technical Director:
JOHN SCOTT-TAGGART,
F.Inst.P., A.M.I.E.E.

EDITOR:
PERCY W. HARRIS, M.I.R.E.
Editorial Telephone: CITY 9911.

Research Editor:
MAJOR JAMES ROBINSON,
D.Sc. Ph.D., F.Inst.P.

PRICE 2d.   SATURDAY, OCTOBER 3, 1925.   Vol. I. No. 3.

BESTWAY
161
The Guide for
HOW TO MAKE
Crystal

CONTENTS

THE HOME-CONSTRUCTOR'S FIRST CRYSTAL SET

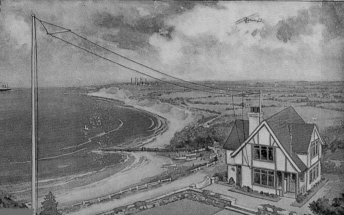

PRICE 2/
RADIO FOR THE MILLION
THE RADIO OWNER'S MAGAZINE

Vol. I., No. 4   September 1927

AUTUMN DOUBLE NUMBER

BESTWAY
162
The Guide for the Wir
HOW TO MAKE
Valve S

THE NEW WIRELESS WEEKLY.   VOL. 1. No. 1. March 21st, 1923.

The RADIOGRAM
3d WEEKLY
AND WIRELESS ANSWERS

The Listener
Published by the British Broadcasting Corporation

Vol. I. No. 1   JANUARY 16, 1929   [Registered at the G.P.O. as a Newspaper]   TWOPENCE

Principal Contents

CONTENTS

A PICTORIAL BLUE PRINT FREE WITH THIS ISSUE

How to Build
A ONE-VALVE SET
Step-by-step details for making a simple but efficient Receiver
By P. R. Bird

How to Construct
A ONE-BATTERY RECEIVER
A "Unidyne" Set which requires no L.T.
By G. V. Dowding, Grad. I.E.E., A.C.G.I

How to Make
A TWO-VALVE LOUD-SPEAKER SET

A ONE-VALVE REFLEX SET
By K. D. Rogers

A TWO-VALVE REFLEX RECEIVER
(Special Pictorial Blue Print with this Article)
By Laurence J. Pritchard

LISTEN IN

MADE IN ENGLAND

RADIO RACE
I.M. SERIES.
MADE IN ENGLAND
RADIO PARIS FRANCE
BERLIN GERMANY
OSLO
BERLIN
RADIO PARIS
MADRID
MADRID SPAIN
ROME ITALY
REGISTERED DESIGN COPYRIGHT.

The Great Wireless Game
LISTEN-IN
MADE IN ENGLAND
BRITISH MANUFACTURE

STERLING No. 1.
CRYSTAL W/T
RECEIVING SET.

The Sterling No. 1 Crystal Receiver has been specially designed for use in connection with the Wireless Telephony Broadcasting scheme, and is suitable for a range of about 25 miles.

RADIO
THE NEW GAME
THE GAME THAT PLEASES

THE RADIO PUZZLER
DIRECTIONS

OSCILLATION
BRITISH BROADCASTING CORPORATION

There are regrettably some who make whistling noises in their loud speakers in order to produce amusement.

ALL ABOUT
THE B.B.C
by 'Ariel'

LISTENIN'!
"Stand by — It's only me!"

'POPULAR WIRELESS' GIFT SUPPLEMENT. Week ending OCT. 25, 1924.

OSCILLATIONS GO BACK 3 SPACES
JAMMED GO BACK 3 SPACES
THUNDER STORM GO BACK 5 SPACES
VALVE TROUBLE GO BACK TO NEW YORK
JAMMED GO BACK 3 SPACES
NEW YORK
OSCILLATIONS MISS NEXT TURN
OSCILLATIONS GO BACK 8 SPACES
ATMOSPHERICS GO BACK 5 SPACES
THUNDER STORM GO BACK 5 SPACES
THE HAGUE

Experiments with radio broadcasting had been in progress all through the previous decade, and in February 1922 the first regular transmissions were made by Marconi's Wireless Telegraphy Co, as authorised by the Postmaster General. For a year each Tuesday night, a broadcast was made from a wooden hut in the village of Writtle, Essex. At this time some 8,000 licensed radio operators were able to listen in. By May 1922, further broadcasting stations were opened, at Marconi's head office in London (call sign 2LO) and at Vickers in Manchester (2ZY); Western Electric opened in London in October (2WP). These three stations were merged into the British Broadcasting Company, with the first broadcast made on 14 November 1922. A ten shilling Broadcast licence was required to listen legally.

The novelty of radio inspired a variety of puzzles and board games, where contestants might run into 'valve trouble' or 'oscillation'.

3

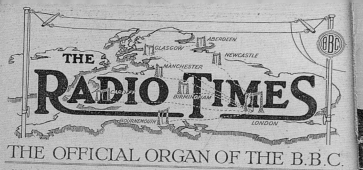

THE OFFICIAL ORGAN OF THE B.B.C.

SANTA CLAUS CALLING!

"JUST A SONG AT TWILIGHT"

It was not long after the BBC was formed that the Radio Times was launched as its 'official organ'. The first issue was dated 28 September 1923, priced at 2d. (a price that remained, apart from larger numbers at Christmas, 6d. and Summer, 3d.). Initially, a page was given to each day's programme listings of the six radio stations: London, Manchester, Newcastle, Birmingham, Cardiff and Glasgow. The circulation of the Radio Times had reached 600,000 in a year, and by 1926 had split into two regional editions. Times varied, but radio programmes commenced in the late morning and closed down before midnight. Mostly for music, there were also programmes for talk and debate and sections for children, women and general news bulletins with a weather report. The Radio Times contained a good selection of articles, but left plenty of space for advertisements on radio equipment or 'fix your aerials with Rawlplugs'. Illustrations and cartoons were an important feature and the best artists were commissioned. While most issues had straightforward black and white covers, special numbers had colourful covers such as those by McKnight Kauffer. In the second BBC Handbook (1929): Why do more than a million buy the Radio Times? Because it is the listeners own paper.

TWO PENCE

...ES
...WEEK

...S BARITZ
...URNIER
...D'ALBE
...OR
...ARJEON
...DGE

...HDAY
...ES

FRENTIS

Radio Times, August 3, 1928. Vol. 20. No. 253. [Registered at the G.P.O. as a Newspaper.] SOUTHERN EDITION.

The RADIO TIMES

SUMMER NUMBER

3d

Radio Times, May 17, 1929. Vol. 23. No. 294. [Registered at the G.P.O. as a Newspaper.] SOUTHERN EDIT

PROGRAMMES FOR MAY 19—MAY 25

THE RADIO TIMES

NEWS

WHITSUNTIDE

E. McK. Kauffer

CONTENTS

(2d)

STORIES   BY   ELINOR MORDAUNT
VERSES   LIAM O'FLAHERTY
AND

SOUTHERN EDITION.

PROGRAMMES.

TIMES

6d.

...S NUMBER

Registered at the G.P.O. as a Newspaper.

Southern Edition.

Price Twopence

TIMES

...casting

Radio Times, December 21st, 1928. SOUTHERN EDITION

RADIO TIMES

6d

CHRISTMAS NUMBER

E. McKNIGHT KAUFFER

Radio Times, September 20, 1929. Vol. 24. No. 312. [Registered at the G.P.O. as a Newspaper.] SOUTHERN EDITION.

THE RADIO TIMES

2d.

THE RADIO TIMES
THE JOURNAL OF THE BRITISH BROADCASTING CORPORATION

Programmes for September 22— September 28

RADIO EXHIBITION NUMBER

A Special Article

Hagedorn

THE

B.B.C
HANDBOOK

E. McK. Kauffer

B.B.C!
HANDBOOK
1929

McK. Kauffer 27

Radio Times, August 2, 1929. Vol. 24. No. 300. [Registered at the G.P.O. as a Newspaper.] SOUTHERN EDITION.

RADIO TIMES

3d.

SUMMER NUMBER

Hagedorn.

THE ILLUSTRATED LONDON NEWS

SHARP'S
SUPER-KREEM
TOFFEE
A Right Royal Favourite

SHARP'S
SUPER-KREEM
TOFFEE

H.R.H.PRINCESS MARY

H.R.H. THE DUKE OF YORK.

LADY ELIZABETH BOWES-LYON

NG NUMBER

PUBLISHING OFFICE, 172, STRAND, LONDON, W.C.2.

FRIDAY, APRIL 27, 1923

LONG LIFE AND HAPPINESS !

Christmas Greetings

"Our Prince"
Set.

The Popular *Prince* FOUNTAIN PEN
Lever Self Filling (FULLY GUARANTEED)

In the early Twenties, two royal
marriages were held at Westminster
Abbey, breaking the tradition of
royal weddings at Windsor Castle.
On 28 February 1922, King George's
only daughter married Viscount
Lascelles. Souvenirs included toffee
tins from Sharp's and Mackintosh (above).
A year later, on 26 April 1923, the
Duke of York married Elizabeth
Bowes-Lyon. A million people watched
the procession. Their visit to Australia
in 1927 was marked by a tin for Hall's
Duchess Assortment that showed
HMS Renown (centre). On 21 April 1926
Princess Elizabeth was born,
joining her mother on the lid of
Meltis chocolate boxes. The
Duchess of York had become one
of the decade's society beauties.
The Prince of Wales was also a
popular figure, and he charmed
the nation. His smiling face
appeared on fountain pens to
cracker boxes, cigarettes (see
p.9) to chocolates box lids (p.3):
this image had been taken from
a photograph while on tour in
Canada during 1919, but the
cigarette he was smoking
36. had been removed.

EDMONDSON'S
RED
SEAL
TOFFEE

OUR CHARMING PRINCE

H.R.H. PRINCE OF WALES.

TOM SMITH'S CRACKERS

GRAPHIC

WEDDING NUMBER

PRICE TWO SHILLINGS

Faulders "ROYAL" Assortment CHOCOLATE

Meltis DUCHESS OF YORK Assorted Chocolates
BEDFORD & LONDON, ENGLAND. HALF POUND (INCLUDING FO

Meltis DUCHESS of YORK Assorted Chocolates
BEDFORD & LONDON, ENGLAND. HALF POUND

RICHMOND

WESTMINSTER ABBEY, APRIL

BUCKING

Daily MIR
THE DAILY PICTURE NEWSPAPER WITH THE LARGEST NET SALE
No. 7,029 SATURDAY, MAY 22, 1926 One Penny

FIRST PICTURE OF THE DUCHESS AND HER BABY

Meltis LITTLE PRINCESS Assorted Chocolates
LTD. BEDFORD & LONDON, ENGLAND.
HALF POUND (INCLUDING FOILS)

Meltis DUCHESS of YORK Assorted Chocolates
LTD. BEDFORD & LONDON, ENGLAND.
ONE (INCLUDING

of the Duchess of York and her baby daughter. The
week in the private chapel at Buckingham Palace, and
Duchess of York Alexandra, after the late
the Queen. Born at 17, Bruton-street, Mayfair,

BABY'S PLATE

Windsor Castle TOM SMITHS
PRINCESS CRACKERS
322. Buckingham Palace
MANUFACTURED IN ENGLAND BY TOM SMITH & Co. LTD LON

OUR EMPIRE'S LITTLE PRINCESS
BORN APRIL 21ST 1926.

H.R.H. PRINCESS ELIZABETH
BORN APRIL 21ST 1926.

A proposal to stage an Empire exhibition was initially made in 1913, and then revived after the Great War. The Empire Stadium, designed by Sir Owen Williams, had to be completed first, since it was to stage the FA Cup final of 1923. On the occasion a crowd of 210,000 football supporters turned up to see Bolton Wanderers beat West Ham 2-1. With a capacity for 125,000, the crowd overspilled onto the pitch, and the match was delayed for 40 minutes while police restored order. The British Empire Exhibition was opened by George V on 23 April 1924. It was intended to celebrate the virtues of the Empire and portray Britain as the mother country to which every part of the Empire was invited. The opening ceremony was broadcast on radio - the first time for a monarch. The King sent a symbolic telegram to himself, transmitted around the world in 80 seconds (see above). The lion emblem was designed by Herrick.

Most Empire countries were represented at the world's largest exhibition; a 216 acre site with its own rail links, 100 electric cars, and boats to move the crowds. Entrance cost 1/6d. for adults, 9d. for children. Roller coasters, water shute, dodgem cars and scenic railway were all in a 47 acre amusement park. The Canadian Pavilion displayed a model of the Prince of Wales made of butter. Manufacturers had their own stands (see Oxo and Sharps on page 1), sometimes making products on site like Jacobs Marie biscuits. Souvenirs abounded — ashtrays, Liptons tea caddies, toffee tins, Crosfield's miniature packs of Persil to Pinkabolic. By the end of October 1924 17½ million visits had been made (the guide book suggested 'try to arrange at least five visits'). Seen as a success, the exhibition reopened March to October 1925 to make up the financial short fall — a further 9¾ million visits at most these summers only to £1¼ million (now only 39

..THE..

International

The Organ of the Left Wing of the I.L.P.

No. 1.   JUNE 19, 1920.   FORTNIGHTLY—ONE PENNY.

THE TASK BEFORE US. By J. T. Walton Newbold.

It is now more than two and a half years since ... cates resort to armed force in defence of the

THE NEW VOICE. July 15, 1920.

THE TRUTH ABOUT BOLSHEVISM. (See page 8.)

The New Voice

The Journal of the Middle Classes Union.

No. 4. Vol. I.   JULY 15, 1920.   PRICE TWOPENCE, MONTHLY.

WORKERS' DREADNOUGHT.—SATURDAY, September 24th, 1921.

The Irish War.

Workers' Dreadnought

FOR INTERNATIONAL COMMUNISM.

Founded and Edited by SYLVIA PANKHURST.

VOL. VIII.—No. 28.   SATURDAY, SEPTEMBER 24th, 1921.   [Weekly.] PRICE TWOPENCE.

OUR POINT OF VIEW

By SYLVIA PANKHURST.

THE COMMUNIST, February 12, 1921.

THE COMMUNIST

An Organ of the Third (Communist) International—

(PUBLISHED BY THE EXECUTIVE COMMITTEE OF THE COMMUNIST PARTY OF GREAT BRITAIN)

No. 28   SATURDAY, FEBRUARY 12th, 1921   [Registered at the G.P.O. as a Newspaper]   TWOPENCE

NOTES OF THE WEEK

COMMUNIST CARTOONS

By ESPOIR & Others

PUBLISHED BY THE COMMUNIST PARTY OF GREAT BRITAIN

THE COMMUNIST REVIEW

No. 1 MAY 1921   6d

THE SPUR

TO THE COMMUNIST REPUBLIC.

Edited and Published by Rose Witcop, at 17 Richmond Gardens, Shepherd's Bush, London, W.12, to whom all communications should be addressed. Annual Subscription, 3s.

Vol. VII.—No. 7.   FEBRUARY, 1921.   [TWOPENCE.

CECIL MALONE

(By GUY A. ALDRED)

THE WORKERS' Republic

The Official Organ of The Communist Party of Ireland.

(An Organ of the Third International.)

Registered as a Newspaper

Founded by James Connolly, August 1898.

Vol. I. No. 6. New Series.   Saturday, November 12, 1921.   Price TWOPENCE.

NOTES ON THE FRONT.

By SPAILPIN OG.

Be "Moderate."

By James Connolly.

BRASS BOTTLE.

The Monarchist

REX DEI GRATIA.

No. 1. Vol. 1.   DECEMBER, 1922.   Price 2d., post free 3d

NOTES

"LOYALTY."

By ROGER MACKARNESS.

Sinn F

Vol 1: No. 1.   TUESDAY, AUGUST 7th,

OURSELVES.

SINN FEIN (WE OURSEL BY THE PRESIDENT

MOSCOW

ORGAN OF THE III CONGRESS OF THE COMMUNIST INTERNATIONAL

Vol 1. No 10. June 4th 1921.

TELEGRAPHIC NEWS.

GERMANY.
Debates in the German Reichstag.

SILESIA.
Situation in Upper Silesia

TURKEY.
Discord Among the Kemalists.

The German Communist Womens' Movement.

THE FORERUNNER OF THE WORKERS' DAILY

THE WORKERS' W

(Incorporating THE COMMUNIST)

OFFICIAL ORGAN OF THE COMMUNIST PARTY OF

No. 1   FEBRUARY 10th, 1923

OUR PROGRAMME

What the "Workers' Weekly" is Out to Fight For

THE AIMS OF THE COMMUNIST PARTY

WHERE IS THE

FIMMEN'S CONFES

Release Hunter

THE MINEWORKER

...IS AN INJURY TO ALL!   WORKERS OF THE WORLD UNITE!

ORGAN OF THE NATIONAL MINERS' MINORITY MOVEMENT.

PUBLISHED FORTNIGHTLY by N. Watkins, Nat. Secretary, 38 Gt. Ormond Street, London, W.C.1, to whom all orders and correspondence should be addressed.   Volume 1. Number 5.   Price : ONE HALFPENNY

MINERS OF GREAT BRITAIN
By A. J. COOK,
General Secretary, Miners' Federation of Great Britain.

The last few weeks has revealed its sectional outlook. The old Agreement must go if the safety and economic security...   We should never put forward proposals for National Agreements that we are not prepared to fight for.

DAILY HERALD
LATE LONDON EDITION

No. 2,488 (No. 1,495—New Series)   LONDON, WEDNESDAY, JANUARY 23, 1924.   ONE PENNY

To-day's Weather — Wind S.E., light or modera e. Rain early, then fairer temporarily mist. Moderate temperature.

FIRST BRITISH LABOUR CABINET

MR. MACDONALD NOW PREMIER
Rapid Developments Follow on Mr. Baldwin's Resignation

AUDIENCES WITH THE KING
Three Peers in the Government : Admiralty Provides a Surprise

WHY CABINET IS LARGE ONE
Plans for Working on Business-like Lines
MEETING TO-DAY
The first meeting of the new Cabinet will be held at 10, Downing-street, at 4 p.m. to-day (writes our Lobby Correspondent). The great, and, I believe, unprecedented promptitude with which the new Cabinet has been announced and is taking over the Administration has created a very favourable impression. The filling up of the Under-Secretaryships is, I am able to state, almost completed, and a full announce...

RAIL STRIKE LEADERS PROPOSE PARLEY
But Managers Insist on Acceptance of Wages Board's Award
"DISCUSS DIFFERENCES"
—Loco Union's Offer
Correspondence passed yesterday between the railway managers and the Associated Society, whose members are on strike. The managers, while prepared to meet the men's agents...

LENIN DIES SUDDENLY
POIGNANT SCENE IN THE SOVIET
A LONG SILENCE
MOSCOW MOURNS GREAT LEADER
Nicolai Lenin (Vladimir Ilyich Oulianoff) died at 6.50 on Monday...

THE YOUNG COMRADE

Vol. 1. No. 5.   AUGUST, 1924   One Halfpenny

...NG WORKER

NOW 1d.

ORGAN OF THE YOUNG COMMUNIST LEAGUE

APRIL 1924   ONE PENNY

STOP THE THIEVING BOSS.

The Worker
Official Organ British Bureau Red International of Labour Unions.

Registered at G.P.O. as a Newspaper.   Acting Editor—A. FERGU...

No. 299   AUGUST 16, 1924   ONE PENNY

DEMAND RELEASE OF CAMPBEL...

The Fly and the Spider's Web.
Engineers Prepare.
By W. HANNINGTON

Walthamstow Stri...
Demand More Milita...
At a mass meeting of the building on strike in Walthamstow the following resolutions were passed unanimously...

Red Star

THE TRUTH ABOUT SOVIET RUSSIA   *Red Star*   A BULLETIN OF RUSSIAN NEWS

FIRST ISSUE   JULY 1927   ONE PENNY

STAND BY WORKERS' RUSSIA !

TORIES PLOTTING WAR AGAINST SOVIET REPUBLIC

WAR ON RUSSIA IS WAR ON YOU !

BULWARK AGAINST BALDWIN

THE breach of relations, both trading and diplomatic, between Great Britain and the U.S.S.R. is mainly due to the two contrasted systems of economy existing in the respective countries. Britain, which is the spearhead of European imperialism, is experiencing a progressive decline, while the Socialist economy of the U.S.S.R. steadily pursues its upward progress.
The contraction of the capitalist world by the withdrawal of U.S.S.R. from the orbit of capitalist economy has intensified the struggle for world markets. The moral support by the U.S.S.R. toward colonial peoples struggling against imperialism, particularly in China, has further contracted British spheres of exploitation.

WHY 20 SPIES WERE SHOT
Soviet Premier Replies to Labour M.P.'s
"PRIMARY DUTY"
Only Bosses and their Allies were "Shocked"

To the telegram received from Lansbury, Maxton, and Brockway protesting against the execution of twenty spies in Russia, Rykoff has replied as follows :—
"Your telegram is apparently due to the publication of the sentence inflicted by the G.P.U. on twenty white guards for organising espionage against the Soviet Union and terror against Soviet leaders.
"Although this sentence was inflicted on active white guard counter-revolutionaries, whose guilt had been proved by documentary evidence, it is widely made use of abroad for rousing public opinion against the Soviet Union. In connection with this sentence innumerable lies and calumnies are being spread through the medium of the foreign press hostile to the proletarian State.

TO HIDE WAR PLANS
"The direct object of this press campaign is the desire to divert at...

BOURNVILLE COCOA
"QUALITY AND FLAVOUR"   MADE UNDER IDEAL CONDITIONS.
See the name "CADBURY" on every piece of Chocolate.

The Labour Woman
Edited by Dr. Marion Phillips

Vol. XIII. No. 2   Price Twopence—Subscription with Postage Three Shillings Annually

---

...UNG MINER...

WOMAN of TO-DAY AND TO-MORROW
THE PAPER EVERY WOMAN SHOULD READ
Vol. 1.   No. 1.

...EKLY

One Penny

...RNATIONAL?
...F FAILURE
...as in 1914"
...ND TREACHERY

The Workers are looking on helpless at an act of war involving half Europe again. The revolt out in bloody conflict. The final act, leading to the end of...

...advance, the International Communist movement held its Council of Action in Essen itself, the centre of the storm area. The revolt out in bloody conflict...

Price 1d.

the "immediate and terrible war" she threatened, England found another way. Her traditional policy of "divide and conquer," inveigled her side too many of the people...

OFFICE WORKER
Monthly Journal for Working Wo...

The Twenties was a time of political extremes. Unemployment rose to a million in 1921 and then doubled by the end of the year. The Russian Revolution under Lenin and Trotsky had brought about a communist state in 1917. The Communist Party of Great Britain was formed in 1920, and a plethora of left-wing publications followed. In 1922 the provisional Irish parliament accepted a treaty with Britain to set up the Irish Free State. Ulster remained part of the UK. Ramsay McDonald became Britain's first Labour Prime Minister in 1924; the same year that ex Tory MP Oswald Mosley joined Labour, Stalin took over on the death of Lenin, Mussolini's Fascists came to power in Italy, and Hitler's Nazi party began to gain support. Two right wing publications were short-lived: The Monarchist and Conservatives' Woman of Today.

Workers' Weekly — No. 169 — FRIDAY, APRIL 30, 1926 — One Penny

Workers' Weekly

Workers of the World, Unite!

The Forerunner of the Workers' Daily.

Push our little
COMPETITION
in aid of our £1,000 Fund

The Workers will Not Fail the Miners

FATE OF WORKERS IN THE BALANCE

Miners Are Facing Most Critical May Day in History

ISSUE IS CLEAR

Trade Unions Must Stand Firm or Suffer Another "Black Friday"

TIME IT WAS SHIFTED, TOO!

ENGINEERS WANT UNITY

London Calling for Plan of Co-ordination

A.E.U. HOLDS UP STRIKE PAY

But Big Majority for Drastic Action is Expected

The Brit

Published by His

LONDON, WEDN

No. 1.

FIRST DAY OF GREAT STRIKE

Not So Complete as Hoped by its Promoters

PREMIER'S AUDIENCE OF THE KING

FOOD SUPPLIES
No Hoarding: A Fair Share for Everybody

The Worker

Official Organ of the National Minority Movement
Editor—A. Ferguson.

"THE WORKER," May 1, 1926.

No. 388.   MAY 1, 1926.   ONE PENNY.

MAY DAY MEANS A UNITED FRONT

THE ELEVENTH HOUR— STAND BY THE MINERS

RALEIGH THE ALL-STEEL BICYCLE

The Star

LONDON. SATURDAY. MAY 1, 1926.

FINAL EDN.

No. 11856.   INDEPENDENT OF THE NEWSPAPER TRUSTS.   ONE PENNY.

EDISON BELL WINNER RECORDS

"A STATE OF EMERGENCY."

Proclamation By The King To-day.

GENERAL STRIKE FIXED FOR MIDNIGHT ON MONDAY.

TRADE UNIONS OFFER TO TRANSPORT SUPPLY OF FOODSTUFFS.

DOCKERS' K.C. SPEAKS

Daily Mail

PRICE 1d   NET DAILY SALE OVER ONE MILLION AND THREE QUARTERS.

LOOKING to Mr. BALDWIN to ACT

First Day of General Strike
Food Plans Work Smoothly
Thousands of Volunteers
Strikers' Great Petrol Waste

Yesterday was the first day of the general strike. Volunteers for emergency services are enrolling in large numbers, and the Government's plans are developing smoothly.

Food supplies are normal.

One or two instances of strikers getting out of hand are reported.

Evening Standard

LATE NIGHT FINAL

No. 31,742.   LONDON, SATURDAY, MAY 1, 1926.   ONE PENNY.

PINOLI'S

GENERAL STRIKE ORDERE

COMPLETE HOLD-UP AT MONDAY MIDNIGHT OF TRAFFIC AND OTHER SERVICES.

TROOPS MOV TO STRIKE ARE

SOUTH WALES, LANCASHI AND SCOTLAND.

Emergency Bulletin.

LATE NIGHT FINAL

THURSDAY MAY 6th

No. 3.

Latest Strike News

THE EVENING STANDA

WEATHER FORECAST: Wind S.W. moderate to fresh. Showe

No. 31747.   LONDON, FRIDAY, May 7, 1926.

A DAY NEARER FAILURE.

There is no immediate prospect of a collapse of the str

DAILY EXPRESS

No. 8122.   LONDON, FRIDAY, MAY 7th, 1926.   ONE PENNY.

FULHAM PALACE as TREATY HOUSE
OFFER FOR STRIKE NEGOTIATIONS

THE INEVITABLE END.
By now the majority of the strikers recognise that failure is upon them.

STRIKERS RETURN TO WORK
MANY MEN RESUME DUTY IN THE PROVINCES

Daily Express

BOOTH'S
There never was — There never will be — A Purer Gin

NO. 8,119.   LONDON, TUESDAY, MAY 4, 1926.   ONE PENNY.

TO-DAY'S WEATHER. Fair to cloudy.

SORE THROAT — CONDY'S FLUID

MOMENTOUS GENERAL STRIKE BEGINS

COMPLETE STOPPAGE.
LAST EFFORTS PROVE FUTILE.

Mr. BALDWIN'S EMOTION.
"ALL I CARE FOR IS BEING SMASHED TO BITS."

TROOPS ON THE MARCH.
BATTLESHIPS IN THE MERSEY.
SEDITION WARNING.

THE STATE TAKES CONTROL.
POWERS OF SEARCH, SEIZURE—

ATTEMPT TO STOP BROADCAST NEWS.
ELECTRICAL UNION'S ANNOUNCEMENT.
OSCILLATION.

The Birmingham

Friday May 7th 1926

STRIKE BULLETIN

1.

THE GENERAL POSITION

DAILY HERALD

LATE LONDON EDITION

BISHOPS AND JUSTICE FOR MINERS (See Page Seven)

No. 3,194 (No. 2,201—New Series)   LONDON, TUESDAY, MAY 4, 1926.   ONE PENNY

To-Day's Weather: Wind between E. and N.E., fair to cloudy; moderate temperature.

Great National Strike Started At Midnight

TRANSPORT, POWER, PRESS AND OTHER WORKERS STOP

Biggest Industrial Dispute in Country's History : A Fight for Miners' Right to Live

"STAND FIRM AND WE SHALL WIN"

General Council's Final Message to Rank and File: Labour's One Aim — Be Loyal,

EVERYONE MAY BE ARRESTED!
Police Powers Under the Emergency Act
SUSPICION ENOUGH
Text of Regulations Issued Yesterday

DAILY GRAPHI

STRIKE EMERGENCY EDITION

SATURDAY, MAY 8, 1926.

No. 11344

THE SPIRIT OF GOOD WILL

Gazette

Stationery Office.

MAY 5, 1926.   ONE PENNY.

COMMUNIST LEADER ARRESTED

Mr. Saklatvala, M.P., Charged at Bow Street

SEQUEL TO MAY DAY SPEECH

THE "BRITISH GAZETTE" AND ITS OBJECTS

Reply to Strike Makers Paralyse Public Opinion

REAL MEANING OF THE

Conflict Between Trade Unions and Parliament

DAILY MAIL was not Printed.

Mirror

BULLETIN

May, May 5th, 1926.   Price—One Penny.

THE PREMIER SEES THE KING.

The Cabinet met yesterday morning.

The Observer.

(ESTABLISHED 1791)

No. 7041.   SUNDAY, May 9th. 1926.

A few words are needed to explain the appearance of the "British Gazette."

There are at present two quite distinct disputes in the country.

THE DAILY MIRROR, Monday, May 17, 1926.

LONDON DAILY PAPERS AS USUAL TO-MORROW

Daily Mirror

THE DAILY PICTURE NEWSPAPER WITH THE LARGEST NET SALE

PROPOSALS FOR NEW STRIKE LEGISLATION

No. 7,024   Registered at the G.P.O. As a Newspaper   MONDAY, MAY 17, 1926   One Penny

THE DOCKERS RETURN TO WORK THIS MORNING

JIM LILLYWHITE AND THE FIRST TEST GAMES.

DAILY GRAPHIC

No. 11,351 ...   Registered as a Newspaper   MONDAY, MAY 17, 1926.   ONE PENNY.

THE OLDEST PICTURE NEWSPAPER IN GREAT BRITAIN.

BACK TO WORK AGAIN.

PRINCE

The Daily Telegraph

FOURTH STRIKE ISSUE.   PRICE TWOPENCE

MONDAY, MAY 10th. 1926.

THE PRIME MINISTER TO THE NATION.

A Striking Pronouncement.

Doors to Peace Open.

"No Surrender of the Constitution."

SPECIAL STRIKE ISSUE.

The Daily Chronicle

No. 20,920.   TUESDAY, MAY 11, 1926.   ONE PENNY.

UNOFFICIAL PEACE MOVE.

Mr. Cook REPUDIATES SUGGESTION OF LOWER WAGES FOR MINERS.

THE LIBERAL POINT OF VIEW.

GET BACK TO PEACE.

CHRISTIAN CHURCHES APPEAL FOR PEACE.

RECEPTION OF THE ARCHBISHOP'S MANIFESTO.

REPORTS IN BRITISH GAZETTE.

Mr. Lloyd George's QUESTION IN THE COMMONS.

DAILY SKETCH

Railway Strike to go on: Official

LONDON, FRIDAY, MAY 14th. 1926.   ONE PENNY.

AFTER-THE-STRIKE SCENES

The Daily Telegraph

STRIKE BULLETIN.

May 8th, 1926.   One Penny.

THE GENERAL POSITION.

nced officially on behalf of the Government yesterday n had not changed since the previous day. As far as concerned there had been nothing very serious and the ble to cope with the situation.

in the 74 London power stations is quite satisfactory n of Battersea, Bermondsey, Poplar, Stepney and West s not quite normal, but in no case is the generation of entirely.

ave been recruited in London and the Home up to practically 75,000.

rable improvement in the railway services running. The G.W.R. ran in all 200 passenger

ONE PENNY TO PAY NO MORE.

freely distributed in Cardiff. Attempts to prevent the trams being run by volunpersed by the police.

e docks still goes on, and no serious inrespect of transport. Sixty per cent of the now running.

is reported from the Midlands and all in division, where essential services are being

attempt to hold up trains, but the police rowd.

are at work in Southampton, and a number of in the Somerset area are inquiring whether

---

THE GENERAL GAZETTE.

A BULLETIN OF 'BUS AND GENERAL NEWS OF THE EMERGENCY PERIOD.

THE SINISTER SLUG.

PRINTED AND PUBLISHED AT THE CHISW... DEPÔT OF THE L...

The British Gazette

COMPLETE REPRODUCTION IN MINIATURE

A SOUVENIR OF THE GENERAL STRIKE

Daily News

AND

The Star

LATE MORNING EDITION

The "Daily News" and "The Star" will resume normal size as soon as possible

POST THIS TO A FRIEND IN THE COUNTRY.

ONE PENNY

THURSDAY, MAY 13, 1926.

GENERAL STRIKE CALLED OFF.

END OF NATIONAL HOLD-UP.

SIR H. SAMUEL'S TRUCE TERMS ACCEPTED.

UNBENDING MINERS.

The King's Appeal.

The following message from the King was broadcast by the B.R.C. last evening:—

"To my People.—The nation has just passed through a period of extreme anxiety... it was to-day announced that the General Strike had been brought to an end. At such a moment it is supremely important to bring together all my people to conduct the difficulty together which still remains.

"This task requires the co-operation of all the and well-disposed men in the country. Even with such help it will be difficult; but it will not be impossible.

"Let us forget whatever element of bitterness the past few days have created..."

POINTS IN THE TERMS.

SUBSIDY TO CONTINUE DURING NEGOTIATIONS.

RE-ORGANISATION GUARANTEE BEFORE WAGE REVISION.

GENERAL STRIKE 1926

LONDON GENERAL OMNIBUS COMPANY LIMITED

THE COMPANY wish heartily to thank

Miss Boland

who acted as Canteen Worker during the General Strike, 4th to 14th May, 1926, for her services in maintaining London traffic and thereby coming to the support of the Country in a serious crisis.

STAFF OFFICER

GENERAL

CHAIRMAN

Travelling around London by motor-bus, tram or underground was encouraged by a continuous supply of maps and leaflets, suggesting places to visit along with the necessary timetables. Whether Easter, Whitsun or August Bank Holiday, there was a place to see or visit, a route and a cheap return ticket — Epping Forest, Windsor, Watford, Chipstead Valley or Chertsey. During weekdays in the early 1920s, a special fare on tramcars was offered in London between 10am and 4pm, which operated at '2d. all the way'. In the 1921 Census, the population of Greater London was 7,480,000.

44.

BY TRAM FROM HAMMERSMITH
WIMBLEDON OR SHEPHERDS BUSH

B.S.A
MOTOR
BICYCLES

B.S.A CYCLES LTD. BIRMINGHAM

CYCLING

Contentment

B·S·A BICYCLES
"Perfect in Every Part"

CURRYS LTD
THE CYCLE PEOPLE

RALEIGH
THE ALL-STEEL BICYCLE

1927

RALEIGH
THE ALL-STEEL BICYCLE

HALFORD
1925 LIST OF CYCLES
ALL BRITISH.

YOUTH   AGE

BUSINESS   PLEASURE

WHEELERGATE,
NOTTINGHAM.

Rudge-Whitworth
Motor Cycles

TYPE L.S. 2-4 h.p.   Cash Prices
without Lamps and Horn £39 0 0
with Lucas Acetylene Lamps and Horn ... £41 0 0
with Bosch Electric Lamps and Bulb Horn ... £47 10 0

"DUNELT" Model "G" Light
Specification as Model

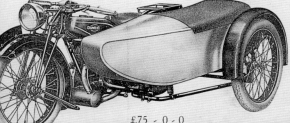

DUNELT
MOTOR CYCLES
1925

"DUNELT"
Model "H"
Tandem Side-car
Combination

All Wheels quickly detachable and interchangeable.

DUNFORD & ELLIOTT (Sheffield) LTD.
BATH STREET   BIRMINGHAM
Telephones : Central 891   Telegrams : "DUNELT Birmingham"

£70 0 0

Including Horn and Licence Holder.

"DUNELT" Model "G" Sports Combination
Specification as Model "G" Solo

Overall length 7ft. 2in.
width 5ft.

£75 0 0

FEBRUARY 24TH, 1927.   THE MOTOR CYCLE.   Advertisements.

Lead the way on a B.S.A.

JANUARY, 1927   PRICE 1/- NET

The BOY'S OWN Paper
THE WORLD'S BEST MAGAZINE FOR BOYS.

RALEIGH
1928

By the mid 1920s there were some six million cyclists, and the number was still on the increase. The cost of a new bicycle was coming down; for instance, a Raleigh gent's model Superbe that cost £20 in 1922 was available for £15 by 1927. By then most new bicycles could be bought for £4 to £12. Cycles were used for going to work, for shop deliveries, for a 'spin' in the countryside, and for cycle racing on road or track. The Cycling magazine was full of reports on racing championships, as well as on 'touring' or the conflict between motorists and cyclists. A cost effective alternative to motoring, the motor cycle could carry a pillion passenger, or with the addition of a tandem side-car, two extra people — and a bowler hat.

47

By the end of the Twenties there were around one million motor cars, three times as many as at the beginning. Open tourers were being overtaken by enclosed and light cars like the Austin Seven (introduced in 1922) and the Morris Minor of 1929 (priced at £135). Prices became lower: the Austin Seven dropped from £225 to just £130. The two-door coupé had also arrived. To combat the growing urban gridlock, automatic traffic lights began to be installed - the first in Wolverhampton in 1928. Children could learn traffic safety through board games (right), which included road signs that had been standardised since the mid 1920s. However, by 1927 there was an average of 14 people dying in road accidents every day.

48.

Motoring was not just about getting from one place to another. It was also a sport, like hill climbing, cross country trials, and competitive motor racing over long distance or circuits such as Brooklands. An enthusiast described the battle of men and machine over nature: 'The gradient as such should defeat few. I doubt if it exceeds 1 in 5. After a preliminary narrow lane one takes a left-hand bend, then the hill stiffens, and a right-hand bend lies ahead. Here the fun begins. The road swings comparatively gently to the right, but the surface is naughty. It is soft to some depth, and this section is liable to be cut up in a not altogether pleasant fashion in view of the possibilities of wheel spin. Clutch and throttle work will play their part here'.

AN ALL BRITISH TRIUMPH
207 Miles per Hour!
THE HIGHEST SPEED EVER ATTAINED ON LAND!

On March 29th 1927, Major H. O. D. Segrave, driving a Sunbeam Car lubricated with Wakefield Castrol, broke World's Records for 1 Kilometre, 5 Kilometres and 1 Mile, reaching a speed of over 207 m.p.h. one way of the course.

SUNBEAM

Using
WAKEFIELD Castrol MOTOR OIL

N. Humphries 27

The Golden Arrow!

azing racing
ar is at this
being built
or Segrave
ort man to
at speed of
es an hour
d. Our
expert
you some
things
this enor-
ar, which
ill travel at
an four
minute!

This photo would make a good teaser in a "What-Is-It?" competition! It is a front view of the Golden Arrow, perhaps the most wonderful racing car ever designed!

Reproduced by courtesy of "The Motor."

t speed king to take off with his new machine which an Captain Malcolm Campbell expects to

The MODERN BOY
EVERY MONDAY.
Week Ending December 8th, 1928. No. 44. Vol. 2.

HE FOUR MILES A MINUTE CAR!

3½ Miles a Minute at Daytona | All about the World's Record Motor Race

The MODERN BOY
EVERY MONDAY
Week ending March 3rd, 1928. No. 4. Vol. 1.
2d

FREE WITHIN! A FINE COLOURED METAL MODEL OF THE WORLD'S RECORD-BREAKING CAR MAJ. SEGRAVE'S 1000 H.P. "Sunbeam"

SUNBEAM

Britain's Speed Champion

The Holder of the World's Land Speed Record, and his Wonderful Car!

Capt. Malcolm Campbell's Record Breaker "BLUE BIRD" 206.9 Miles Per Hour.
Next Week in The Famous L.M.S.R. Express Engine "Royal Scot"

TRAVELLING SOME — 100 YARDS A SECOND.

SPEED.

A VIVID DESCRIPTION OF THE MIGHTY POWER OF CAPTAIN MALCOLM CAMPBELL'S "BLUE BIRD," WHICH FORMS THE SUBJECT OF THIS WEEK'S GRAND FREE

The MODERN BOY
EVERY MONDAY.
Week ending March 10th, 1928. No. 5. Vol. 1.
2d

Britain's Speed Champion!

NEW SCHOOL SERIES·NEW SER

Stories by SIR ALAN COBHAM, GUNBY HADATH, etc

The GEM
2d LIBRARY
EVERY WEDNESDAY
No. 1,069. Vol. XXXIV. August 11th, 19

The Car That Made History — MALCOLM CAMPBELL'S "BLUE-BIRD"

FREE TOPPING COLOURED METAL MODEL INSIDE

THE NELSON LEE LIBRARY
2d
DON'T MISS NEXT WEEK'S RECORD-BREAKING FREE GIFT!

REAL METAL MODEL OF WORLD'S FASTEST CAR
FREE GIFT NEXT WEEK
New Series No. 81. OUT ON WEDNESDAY. November 19th, 19

THE NELSON LEE LIBRARY
2d
THE RECORD BREAKER 1000 H.P. 207 M.P.H

REAL METAL MODEL OF WORLD'S FASTEST CAR
GIVEN FREE WITH THIS ISSUE
New Series No. 82. OUT ON WEDNESDAY. November 26th, 19

THE NELSON LEE LIBRARY
2d
THE WORLD-FAMOUS RACING CAR "BABS"

REAL METAL MODEL GIVEN FREE WITH THIS ISSUE
New Series No. 82. OUT ON WEDNESDAY. December 10th, 19

Motor racing made good board games; record breaking speed attempts were right for the cover of boy's story papers - a combination of danger and heroism. For instance, the racing car 'Babs' (above) was thought capable of reaching 200 mph. But when speeding at 180 mph over Pendine Sands in Wales, one of the driving chains snapped and the driver, Parry Thomas was killed instantly: 'A noble end for a noble British car and a fearless, gallant Britisher!' The main contenders for the land speed record were Henry Seagrave and Malcolm Campbell. Seagrave was the first man to reach 200 mph when his red Sunbeam clocked 204 mph on Daytona Beach, Florida, in March 1927. (The Castrol advert above boasts a speed of 207 mph for one stretch). This easily broke Campbell's record of 174 mph set the previous month with his Blue Bird car racing over the sands in Wales; but Campbell came back in a revamped Blue Bird to reach 206.9 mph in February 1928. Meanwhile, Seagrave had a new car, the Golden Arrow (see left), and in March 1929 he reached 231 mph: that was almost four miles a minute.

Commercial passenger flights had begun in 1919 with Handley Page, flying to Paris and Brussels. Supported by the government, Imperial Airways was formed in 1924, not just to fly to Europe, but eventually to the Empire countries. In 1929 a trip to Karachi was possible, though some of its route was by train. Most European countries had their airlines, as listed in the International Aerial Time Table of 1929, and Australia, the USA and Canada had fledgling services. But the romance of the air was as much reflected in the air pageants and RAF displays - or for two guineas, tea in the air over London. Intrepid aviators included Alan Cobham (Australia and back in 1926) and the American Charles Lindberg (solo across the Atlantic New York to Paris in 1927), and in 1929 the British Supermarine Napier seaplane won the Schneider Trophy with a time of 283 mph, watched by two million spectators. Problems dogged British airships. Nevertheless, at the end of 1929 the R100 and R101 were built, the latter being the world's largest airship - the fate of commercial airships was in their hands.

52.

CANADIAN PACIFIC

TO CANADA & U.S.A
ONLY FOUR DAYS OPEN SEA

HAPAG

GESELLSCHAFTS REISEN 1928

The French Riviera
The Town of Flowers, Sports, and Fashion

CANNES

SEASON FROM OCTOBER TO MAY

GOLF · TENNIS · POLO · YACHTING
RACING · HORSE SHOWS
AND BATTLES OF FLOWERS
The Touring Centre of the Riviera
MUNICIPAL CASINO
and Théâtre
Enquiry Office · SYNDICAT D'INITIATIVE

How to see Europe from an Armchair

AUSTRALIA CALLS YOU

California for the Tourist

California for the Tourist

Southern Pacific

Southern Pacific

MITTELMEER FAHRTEN
Frühjahr 1927

Switzerland
PUBLISHED BY THE
SWISS FEDERAL RAILWAY
BERNE
PRINTED IN SWITZERLAND

THE SUMMER-TIME RIVIERA

French Line

French Line
THIRD CLASS

The
TRIUMPHANT
TRIO
ILE de FRANCE
PARIS
FRANCE

TO AUSTRALIA

SAILING AND FARE LIST
AUSTRALIAN COMMONWEALTH
LINE OF STEAMERS
FOR FURTHER INFORMATION APPLY TO AUSTRALIA HOUSE, STRAND, LONDON, W.C.2
AGENCIES THROUGHOUT GREAT BRITAIN AND IRELAND

1925 OFF THE BEATEN TRACK BY THE 1925
FINLAND LINE
An Invigorating & Inexpensive
HOLIDAY AFLOAT.
£19.10.0 12 DAYS £19.10.0

CUNARD ATLANTIC HOLIDAYS

CANADIAN PACIFIC

R·M·S·P

P&O CRUISES, 1929

CANADIAN PACIFIC

HOLIDAY TOURS TO CANADA & U.S.A.

TO CANADA & U.S.A.
THIRD CLASS

1st JULY to 30th SEPTEMBER, 1923.
SOUTHERN RAILWAY COMPANY (South Western Section).
London & South Western Railway
TO THE
CHANNEL ISLANDS
AND THE CONTINENT
By TURBINE and TWIN SCREW STEAMERS,
Fitted with Wireless Telegraphy.

CHEAPEST AND MOST COMFORTABLE
Night Route to PARIS, THE RIVIERA,
ITALY AND SWITZERLAND.
Circular Tours through Normandy &
Brittany, Valley of the Loire etc..

The great liners steamed majestically across the oceans, carrying their passengers in comfort around the world. It took five days to sail from Southampton to New York. A return trip to America cost £35, or £70 to Australia. Whilst the French Riviera was a popular winter-time destination, by the end of the 1920s, Cannes, Nice and Monte Carlo were all being promoted as summer resorts. 55.

In 1923 the government restructured the 100+ railway companies into just four major networks. Only Southern Railway opted for electrification on a large scale, so it was mainly the powerful steam locomotives that sped passengers, freight and the Royal Mail across the country. Britain's most powerful engine in 1927 was Southern's The Lord Nelson (see Meccano and Magnet above). The world's most famous express was The Flying Scotsman, built in 1922; from 1928 it travelled non-stop from King's Cross to Edinburgh. The Royal Scot began its regular route from Euston to Glasgow via Carlisle in 1927.

ELECTRIFICATION!

700 MILES OF SOUTHERN RAIL-
WAY WILL BE ELECTRIFIED BY
SPRING NEXT YEAR ~ 3 NEW
SECTIONS OPEN THIS SUMMER
~ 3 ELECTRIC FOR EVERY STEAM
TRAIN NOW RUNNING ~ ~ ~
~ TOTAL COST £8,000,000

WORLD'S GREATEST SUBURBAN
ELECTRIC

SOUTHERN

PACKED WITH COMIC PICTURES

FOR BOYS AND GIRLS

THE SEASIDE COMIC 2d

MILLY AND BILLY GO TO SEA

And the Jungle Boys Take a Dip in the Briny!

SCARBOROUGH

THE QUEEN OF WATERING PLACES

HOW TO SEE GREAT BRITAIN
COOK'S MOTOR COACH TOURS

Travel Greyhound
PIONEERS OF LONG DISTANCE SERVICES

G.B. STERN'S New Novel "REVOLT" COMMENCES INSIDE
HOME Magazine

TORQUAY
THE ENGLISH RIVIERA

TANKERTON.
"The more we are together,
The merrier we'll be!"

PROGRAMME
EASTBOURNE

"Further outlook promising!"

Sorry I can't join you to-day —
a Moth has eaten my bathing
dress.

We'll soon be in the swim

"PHILOSOPHY MAY BE ALL RIGHT
BUT GIVE ME THE 'BARE FACTS'!"

TANKERTON.
TELL ME MORE!
TELL ME MORE!!
TELL ME MORE!!!

One gust of wind, and they're
ready for bed here!

"Father's under one of these
heaps, but we can't remember
which!"

BROADSTAIRS.
Don't cry darlings! There are plenty of girls

AT CANVEY-ON-SEA

The annual seaside holiday
was the great escape during
the summer — sand castles,
beach balls, parasols, the
traditional donkey ride and
day trips in a charabanc
(see The Popular, centre of page).
As the decade progressed,
bathing costumes were
becoming briefer and more
daring. By 1924, a cartoon ran:
'Flossie: Don't you think this new
one-piece bathing costume
makes girls look shorter?
Maudie: I don't know; but they
certainly make boys look longer.'
Seaside resorts vied for
attention — Southend with the
world's longest pier, Torquay
with its sub-tropical
gardens.

58.

LONDON'S TRAMWAYS

BY TRAM TO THE EMBANKMENT

REIGATE
PRIORY PARK
BY MOTOR BUS

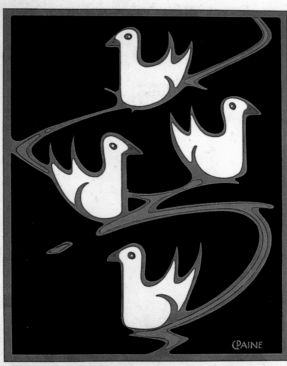

TRAVEL IN COMFORT BY TRAM

LNER FOR FISH

SHEP

CATCH EAST COAST FISH
70% OF FISH EATEN LANDED AT LNER PORTS

CPAINE

KINGSTON BY TRAM

CHARLES PAINE

BARNET BY TRAM

Transport posters reflected the new style of commercial art which became known as Art Deco.

EVENTS of the 1920s

1920
League of Nations created
Communist Party of GB formed
Cenotaph unveiled in Whitehall, London
Moorhouse set motor cycling speed record of 100 mph at Brooklands
Felix the Cat created by Otto Messmer
Rupert Bear appeared in Daily Express
Hornby clockwork trains launched
Smith's Potato Crisps went on sale
Police 'flying squad' formed in London.

1921
British Legion founded: first poppy appeal
Postmen stop making deliveries on Sunday
World's largest airship (R38) built in Britain for US Navy
Car tax discs appeared on windscreens
Chanel No5 available in Britain.

1922
First regular radio service; BBC formed
British troops leave Irish Free State
Tutankamun tomb discovered by Howard Carter
Austin Seven motor car introduced
Wall's Ice Cream launched.

1923
Duke of York married Elizabeth Bowes-Lyon
Radio Times went on sale
FA Cup Final held at Wembley Stadium
Transatlantic wireless broadcast to USA
John Reith appointed managing director of BBC.

1924
British Empire Exhibition opened
Imperial Airways formed
First Labour government took power
Mauretania record crossing of Atlantic (5 days, 90 mins)
First Winter Olympics, held in French Alps
Crossword puzzle published in British newspaper.

1925
BBC reaches audience of 10 million; its education programme heard by over 1,000 schools
Exposition des Arts Décoratifs held in Paris; style became known as Art Deco.

1926
TUC call General Strike
Princess Elizabeth born
Greyhound racing began
First Grand Prix held in Britain, at Brooklands
Alan Cobham flew from London to Cape Town and back (16,000 miles), later Australia and back (28,000).

1927
Seagrave broke land speed record at 204 mph
Charles Lindbergh flew solo New York to Paris
First London to Brighton vintage car rally
Speedway racing began in Britain.

1928
Voting age for women lowered from 30 to 21
Alexander Fleming discovered penicillin
Automatic traffic lights installed, in Wolverhampton
First diesel trains in Britain
Football players with numbers, introduced by Arsenal
Croydon airport opened
£1 and 10 shilling notes came into circulation
Lady Chatterley's Lover by DH Lawrence published in Florence, avoiding UK censorship
First all-talking film shown in London, The Terror, adapted from the Edgar Wallace novel.

1929
Police call boxes introduced
Britain has 1.6 million telephones in use
'I speak your weight' machines introduced
Schneider Trophy won by the British Supermarine S6 seaplane with a time of 283 mph
R100 and R101 airships built and flying
Wall Street crash: 24 October.